I Can Ask For Help

Written by Chemise Taylor

Illustrated by Alexis B. Taylor

Copyright © 2019 by My Skills Books

Published by My Skills Books

All rights reserved. No part of this publication may be reproduced, distributed, or transmitted in any form or by any means, including photocopying, recording, or other electronic or mechanical methods, without the prior written permission of the publisher, except in the case of brief quotations embodied in critical reviews and certain other noncommercial uses permitted by copyright law.

First Printing, 2019.

ISBN: 978-1-951573-00-3

www.myskillsbooks.com

I love to play. I have so much fun,
when I jump around and run.

**Oh No! Oh No! I tripped and fell.
This really hurts, who can I tell.**

I find my mommy. She is on the phone.

Should I tell her what happened or leave her alone?

I go in the room.
No need to delay.

"Excuse me, mommy. I have something to say."

"I ran, I fell and hurt my knee.
It really hurts. Can you help me?"

She says, "Sure thing, little bee, thank you for telling me."

She takes me by the hand and says, "Come and sit down. you were right to come to me. No need to frown."

She cleans my knee and after she is done, she gives me a band-aid and says "Now, be careful when you run."

"Thank you mommy, I don't think I could have done that myself."

She gives me a kiss and says "Glad to help!"

Book Details

Story Word Count: 159

Key Words: Ask, Help, Knee, Play, Mommy, Fell, Phone, Band-Aid

Comprehension Check

- What was the story about?
- What is she speaking to?
- What did she hurt?

Reading Award

This certificate goes to:

_____

for reading "I Can Ask For Help"

Good Job!

More books, apps and resources at myskillsbooks.com

www.ingramcontent.com/pod-product-compliance
Lightning Source LLC
Chambersburg PA
CBHW042108090526

44591CB00004B/50